IKEBANA
Fruits & Vegetables
Toshie Yokoi

SHUFUNOTOMO CO., LTD.
Tokyo, Japan

Second printing, 1988

© Copyright in Japan 1986 by Toshie Yokoi
© Photographs by Eigo Ouchi
Book Designs by Momoyo Nishimura

Published by SHUFUNOTOMO CO., LTD.
2-9, Kanda Surugadai, Chiyoda-ku, Tokyo, 101 Japan

ISBN: 4-07-974446-3
Printed in Japan

IKEBANA
Fruits & Vegetables

FOREWORD

In the highly competitive world of Japanese flower arrangement where hundreds of schools and thousands of teachers vie for recognition and the concomitant financial success, the true ikebana artist may sometimes be unacclaimed. But when one does encounter the works of ikebana artists, perhaps in a chance exhibition or a random book, their genius with flowers is gloriously evident.

Such an artist is Toshie Yokoi whose original approach to the use of fruits and vegetables as ikebana materials titillates the imagination while delighting the eye. My studies with her—the two of us working alone in her studio with materials I had gathered from garden, field and even the green grocers—were hours of complete satisfaction.

May these examples of her work inspire you, to see with her eyes, new possibilities in nature's riches.

Fay Kramer
President Emeritus
Ikebana International

September 1986

PREFACE

It has been believed generally that ikebana, the art of Japanese flower arrangement, is something you learn through lessons with flowers and branches provided from the local florist shop. But when the floral materials cannot be obtained from commercial sources, it does not mean that the pleasures of ikebana cannot be enjoyed, especially with today's ikebana when free style is so popular. The important thing is for each individual to be ingenious in discovering plant materials that they will find satisfying to arrange. I am convinced that abilities like technique, skill and a sense of balance can be acquired and that eventually the talent to make correct judgements will develop. Because ikebana calls for originality, in becoming aware of the potentials of various materials, you may unearth sensitivities long buried within yourself.

What has led me to these conclusions has been my extensive contacts with people living in the farming villages who are kept busy normally with farm work and have no florists within their vicinity. I wanted to share with them my love of ikebana and to open their eyes to the beauties of nature in their own surroundings. For them I originated my own version of ikebana which I called "NŌ-no IKEBANA." The character for the worod "nō" means agriculture as applied to all plant life on the countryside.

In a farming village there are to be found products both cultivated and wild that have excellent possibilities for "NŌ-no IKEBANA." Under my guidance some farm ladies have learned to choose what charms them or arouses their interest so that they can freely arrange as they please. My work of twenty years begins to be in evidence as "NŌ-no IKEBANA" becomes recognized as one of the new cultures of the Japanese farming villages.

I have arranged the following pieces to give some suggestions to those who would like to try a "NŌ-no IKEBANA." You do not have to live in the country to practice it, but just look around you for the unexpected or unusual beauties that abound in nature.

I wish to express my gratitude to Mrs. Fay Kramer for going through the English text and I am greatly indebted to Mr. Kazuhiko Nagai and Mrs. Michiko Kinoshita of Shufunotomo, for their patience and encouragement, and Mr. Eigo Ohuchi for his photographs taken over a period of two decades.

Toshie Yokoi 友誼枝

Toshie Yokoi

CONTENTS

Part III   VEGETABLES: The Triumph of Vegetables,   *63–100*

INTRODUCTION

I have always enjoyed looking at things. Just selecting things when shopping used to be so much fun. Each item seemed to have a character and value of its own which inevitably fascinated me.

These days, however, there are simply too many things around. As a result, not only have we lost our sense of appreciation but our very desire for material things has weakened. Mistaking material abundance for happiness we seem to have lost something important for our lives.

Blessed as we are with the beauty of nature all around us, we seem to have lost our ability to appreciate that beauty. For me, just thinking of prosaic life in the city surrounded by concrete structures, such as sky-scrapers, apartment houses, condominiums, supermarkets, expressways, and underground-shopping malls, makes me shudder. What's worse, I have a feeling I will probably be incased in a concrete grave after I die.

I came to realize the true beauty of the rural setting more than 20 years ago. Ever since then whenever the occasion presented itself I went out of my way to seek materials for my flower arrangements in the countryside. The trouble is, the more I became enchanted with things in their natural setting, the less I was able to satisfy myself with flowers sold in city shops. They are simply not as lively as flowers found in nature and consequently fail to touch our hearts.

My visits to the farm always brought me great peace of mind. I wonder what provoked that feeling in me? I have reached the conclusion that it must come from the deep attachment I sensed on the part of the farmers for the things they grow. I could even detect in the earth and in the air how much they put their very heart and soul into growing things.

I have long wanted to express my gratitude to the farming people and one day an idea came to my mind.

My idea was to make flower arrangements using materials that I have picked up on the farm and then have these arrangements photographed to show to the farmers. As I thought out the idea, plans seemed to develop very easily and I became quite excited about the project. Putting it into practice, however, proved to be a far more difficult matter. To begin with it was not easy for me to travel to rural areas to gather the necessary materials. Even after I did get them, it was not always easy to arrange them exactly the way I wanted. There were times I could not make a timely appointment with the photographer to take a shot of the completed work. With all these problems and headaches, more than once I was so discouraged that I thought of giving up the project entirely.

When I got in these moods, I tried to remember my visits to the farm and the excitment I felt from seeing the beauty of nature all around me.

Even as a child I had fond memories of visiting a farm house on the Tama River in suburban Tokyo. Before the war, we often visited this farm house. It was a large one-story house, standing back from the road, with a beautiful straw-thatched roof. We would usually reject the offer to the inner rooms of the house, preferring to stay in the spacious area at the entrance of the house. Here we would sit on straw mats laid on the dirt floor around the frame of the hearth and enjoy chatting with members of the family. Occasionally we were treated to tasty rice cooked on the log fire in front of us. Our visits to this farm house were indeed heart-warming experiences for us and we felt as though we had returned to a place which was like a spiritual home.

After the war, swept up in the wave of the new age, our living style changed substantially. Even this farm house was not an exception. Gradually changes took place inside and outside the house. It is now a two-story building with all the modern facilities such as a TV set, a refrigerator, a washing machine, a car and of course a telephone. It has, in fact, become another ordinary modern dwelling.

Yet, in the front yard they still grow flowers and they still offer these flowers at the family altar or decorate their rooms with them, adding some richness to their daily life. They might simply be doing these things out of habit without really thinking about it, but I was deeply impressed with those simple flowers from the yard. They reminded me anew of the fact that in rural areas the beauty of nature still exists so abundantly and that it was my mission to make flower arrangements out of simple materials.

Overwhelmed by the thought that the nature which was being destroyed in the city by the advance of material civilization, nevertheless persisted gloriously in the countryside, I visited those places as often as I could to gather materials and then devoted myself to arranging them as an expression of my admiration. But to the farmer's eyes the materials I used were nothing more than a natural part of their environment.

Looking at things from this point of view, everything I saw on the farm, vegetables, fruits, twigs and branches from the neighboring hills, wild flowers from the fields, all became appropriate materials for my flower arrangements.

Although I yearn for such natural materials, unfortunately nature is not to be found near where I live. I urge everyone to try using materials collected directly from nature and to apply new ideas for their flower arrangements. I am sure you will be able to create works that are imaginative and exciting. In so doing you will be promoting a new and different culture of nature.

One time I stayed overnight at a farmhouse to see what it was like to "live close to the soil." What impressed me most when talking with the farmer's wife was the way she mentioned repeatedly how much she enjoyed farming and how happy she was to be a farmer. To me these words were beautiful and I could not help but admire her. The harmonious colors of her hand woven clothes reflected her delightful personality. She made me think about the depth of the meaning of such words as "happiness" and "beauty."

If people feel that they have to buy flowers at the florist's in order to make a flower arrangement, they are grossly mistaken. They should realize that they have an abundance of truly beautiful things each season of the year right in the nature all around them. Using nature's own blessed materials I would urge you to make flower arrangements in a spirit of gratitude to nature. This is the genuine meaning behind the art of flower arranging.

To Farm People Devoted to the Soil:

Part I

FRUITS

Jewels of the Field

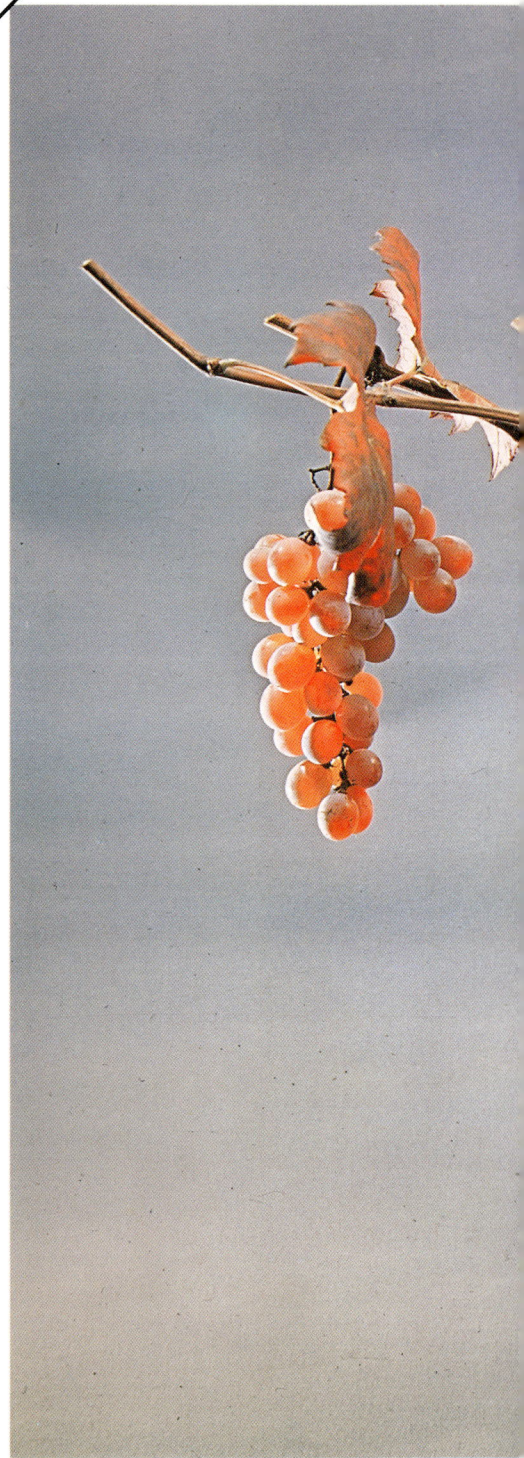

Unlike the usual cultivation of grapes on waist high supports, the grapes in certain areas of Japan are grown on a high trellis. I remember fondly the day when I lay under the framework of vines to get a better view. As far as I could see under the beautiful autumn sky were cluster after cluster of glorious powder coated grapes suspended from above like jeweled chandeliers. I was simply overwhelmed by the actual dream-like beauty of them all.

But all my efforts to catch the spirit of the grapes in an arrangement eluded me, though the owners kindly supplied me with as many bunches as I needed. I wanted to use the grapes from the Yamanashi Prefecture for it was here that my husband as a young agronomy professional had made his first survey. To me the grapes are especially memorable and so when I was able finally to capture them as shown in this picture, my eyes filled with tears as the past welled up within my heart.

Grapes and sunflowers in a beige-colored vase

As a kind of sunshade, I trained grape vines to grow up over my roof. As it turned out I got a bonus as bunches of fine grapes began to ripen. They were ready to burst with juice, the slightest touch would cause a spray of juice. I had so many grapes that I had enough to make

some wine. But what delighted me most was that I could savor the tasty fruit by simply reaching my hand out of the window. The tomatoes are home grown also, so I put them with the grapes.

Grapes and tomatoes in a ceramic vase

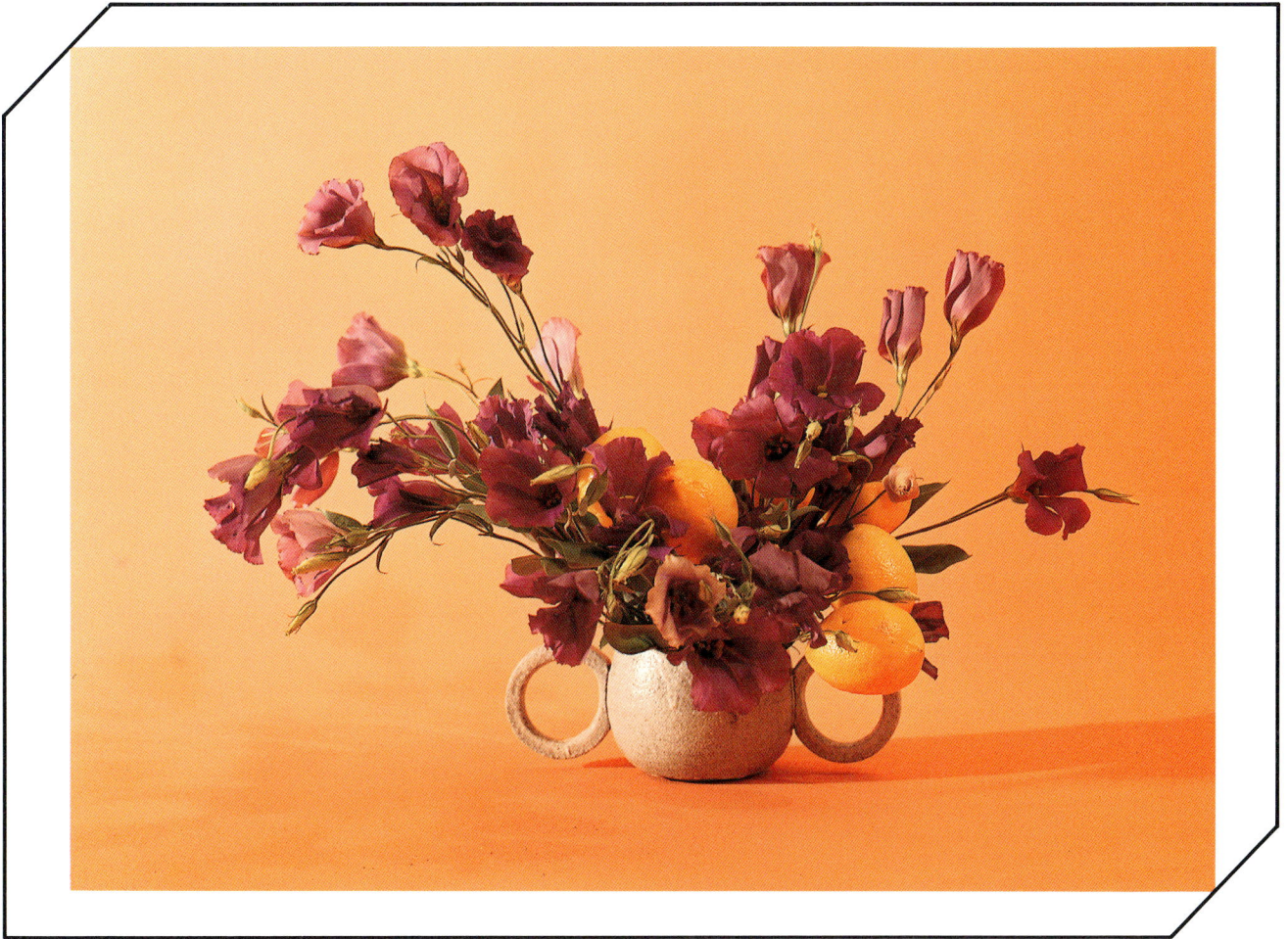

The delicate and fresh scent of the lemon tells us of the gay laughter and pleasant conversation around a table where the guests are treated to homemade pastries. It is a moment in one of those long leisurely afternoons.

Lemon and godetia in a ceramic vase with handles, Banko-yaki

Sweet and delicate peach blossoms give promise of large delicious looking fruit to make our daily life even more enjoyable and happy.

The continuing and uninterrupted growth of the devil's tongue is full of the fresh and productive feeling of the country which seems to seep into our hearts.

Peach and devil's tongue leaves in a ceramic vase, Banko-yaki

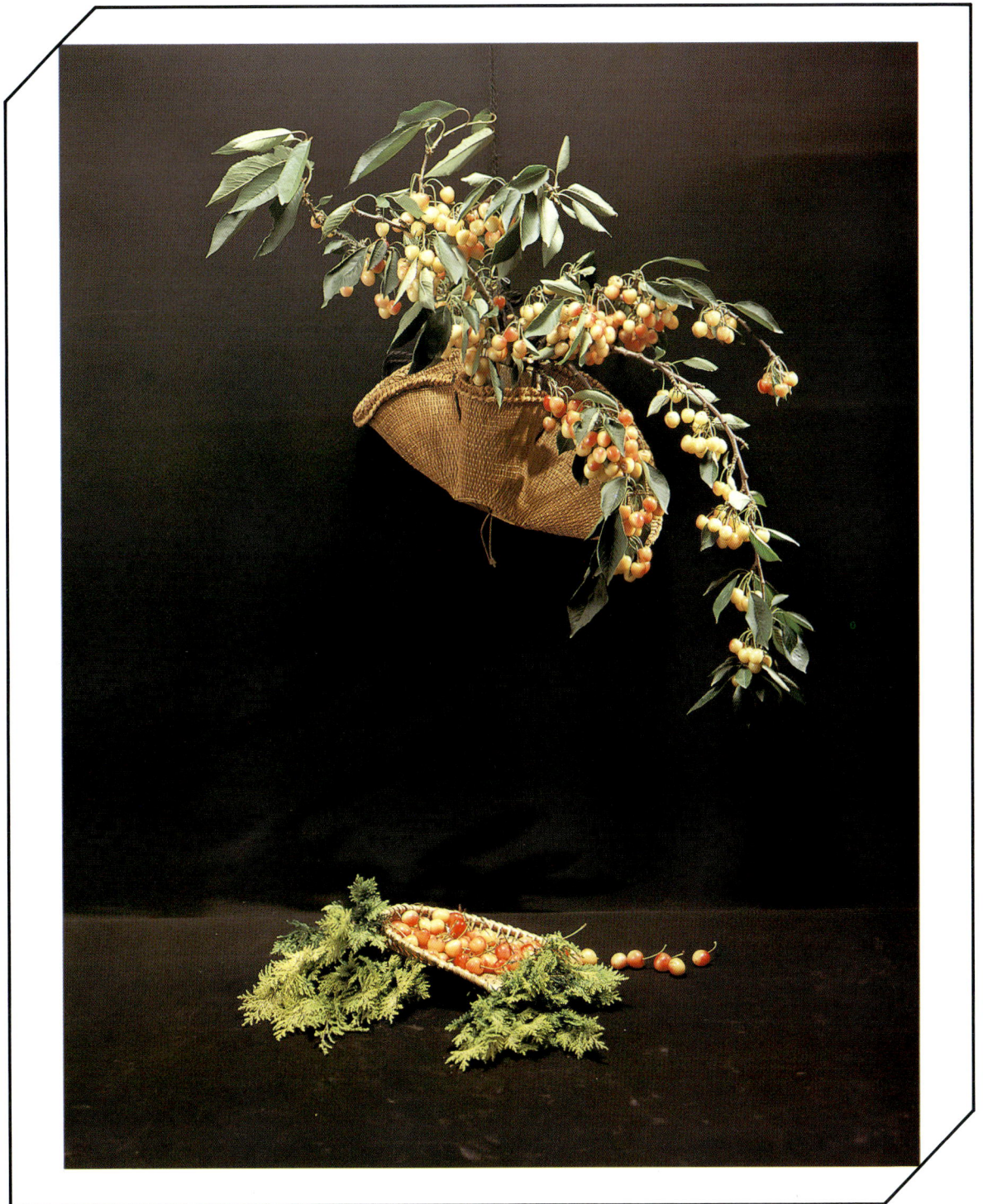

"Abundant cherries drooping on the branches look so beautiful, just like fireworks in the night sky." I uttered these words when I saw them for the first time, and was so deeply moved by them. My impression hasn't changed a bit even though I have viewed the cherries in harvest season many times.

Cherries in a braided rush hat and straw oval platter

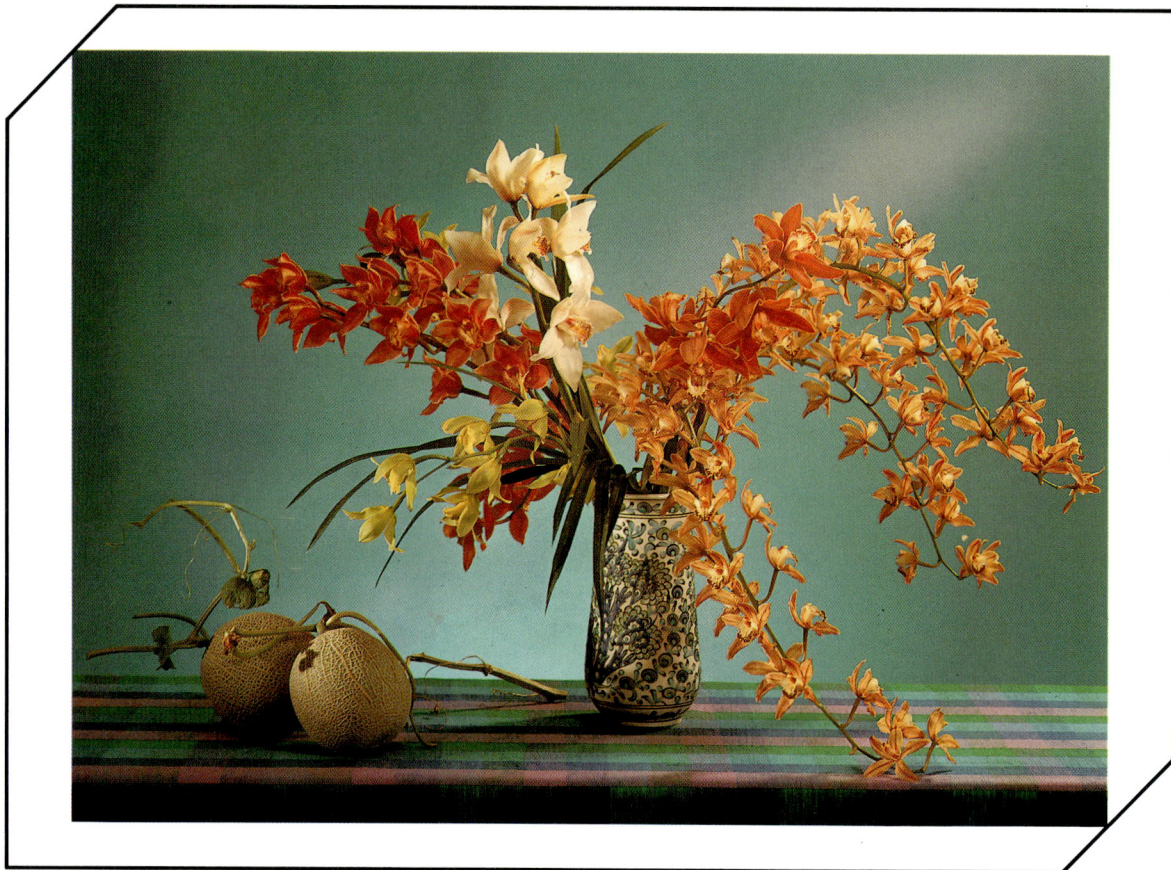

Combining melons and orchids creates a very exotic pairing. Both are greenhouse grown and they come to perfection only through the dedicated care of human hands. Their present beauty shows no signs of any difficulties in their past. The two together join most felicitously in celebrating a happy occasion.
Orchids and melons in a Spanish pot

One day I suddenly hit on the idea of making a visit to a southern island to see their famed pineappple plantations. When I arrived I was disappointed for there was nothing extraor-

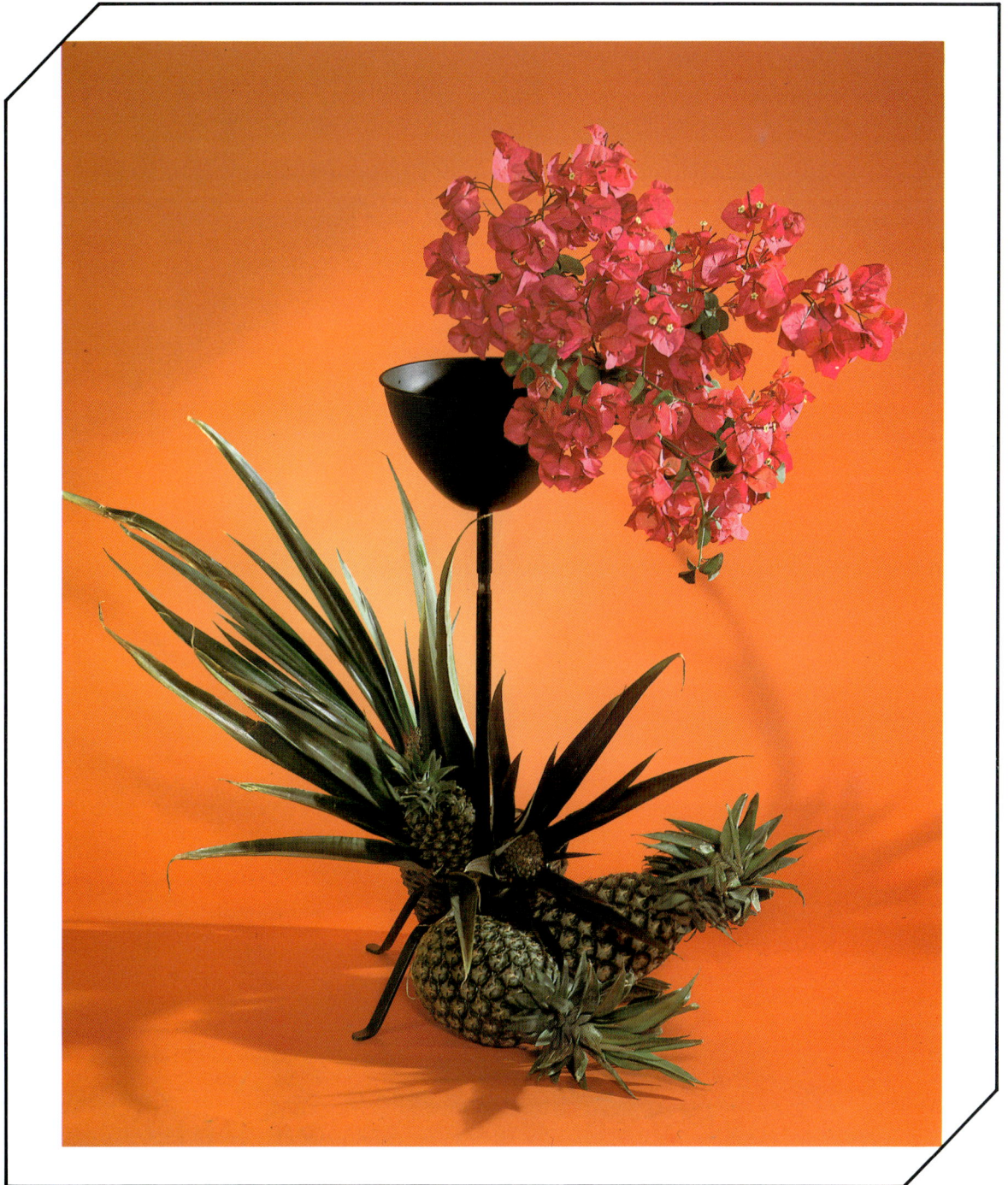

dinary in the monotonous slopes covered with acres of pineapples, growing all the way down to the shoreline. But my enjoyment was raised when I discerned in the distance another shore glittering brilliantly in the sunshine with a stand of bougainvillea.
Pineapple and bougainvillea in an iron compote stand

One rainy day I went to a famous farmhouse for their strawberries. Each plant was sheltered in a vinyl plastic hothouse and as their caretakers, like foster parents, pulled up the sides to peer underneath, they seemed to inquire, "Is everybody well?" The strawberries with bright smiles and brimming vigor, in spite of the rain outside answered, "Yes, we have grown well, thanks to your tender care." As I left their sweet fragrance followed me as a downpour descended and I picked my way along a brook where I came upon some rain soaked pussy willows. Gathering a few to go with the strawberries I admonished the others, "Pull yourselves together, the rain will pass."

Strawberries and pussy willows in a bamboo vase and straw

In a vineyard growing Pione grapes a suffocatingly sweet fragrance dominated the air. Clusters of grapes dangling heavily and abundantly were each wrapped carefully in a transparent milk white vinyl. The picture of the lightly powdered fruit appearing inside the cover was reminiscent of a bride dressed in the traditional Japanese bride's hood. Just as a bride must feel a sense of gratitude toward her parents who had brought her up with such affection to this time of parting, so the grapes must feel toward their caretakers.

Every year on my pilgrimage to the grape country of Kai I am welcomed by the ingenuous faces of the sunflowers, looking their loveliest in the fields to announce the season of the grapes.

Pione grapes and sunflowers on bricks

I did not know anything about the kiwi fruit except that I was fascinated by the taste of it, so I must confess I found quite a few surprising things about it.

I was happy, however, to have reached my own conclusion and to be convinced that these branches, these leaves, and the way these roots spread along can produce such an exquisite taste. I can easily imagine what kind of hard work must be put in to cultivate them.

Kiwi fruit and bougainvillea in a beige vase

The apples have been nurtured with utmost care by the people of the farming village, starting from the pruning of branches in the snow, and then the spraying, followed by much debudding of the blossoms and lastly the young fruit is bagged to protect them during their ripening. And now they look beautiful and are all set for the harvest.

   I was so impressed with everything about the wonderously lovely apples created by nature and human wisdom that I was completely at a loss for words.

Apple in an ash stand for cigarettes

It was only a little while ago when the branches of pomegranates with green leaves were rustling in the breeze, and were telling us, "The real summer is coming soon." Those branches looked as if they had little crimson ribbons tied here and there. Pomegranates were intent, under the bright sunshine, on strenuous physical training at that time when people were panting from heat, and now they have naturally produced fine fruit, and are boasting of the result.

I would like you to take a good look at them ornamenting the field of late autumn with an overwhelmingly vigorous maturity.
Pomegranates in a spool for linen thread

The spirea looks lovely at any time of the four seasons, but it looks outstandingly beautiful in the setting sun with red leaves in the background, and I was captivated by its quiet splendor. At the very same time, the Chinese quince dropped its fruit on the ground, finally unable to hold the weight of them all.

The amiable picture of them and the setting sun still remain in my heart as one of the precious memories of a farming village.

Chinese quince and spirea thunbergii in a ceramic vase

Only the fruit remained on the persimmon trees and all the leaves are gone. The dark branches presented a stark silhouette as they held up the fruit glistening like agate gems high against the autumn skies.

It was difficult to catch the richness in the limits of an ikebana but I settled for this image evoked by a heavily laden persimmon tree from my backyard.

Persimmon and Japanese silverleaf in a brick-colored vase

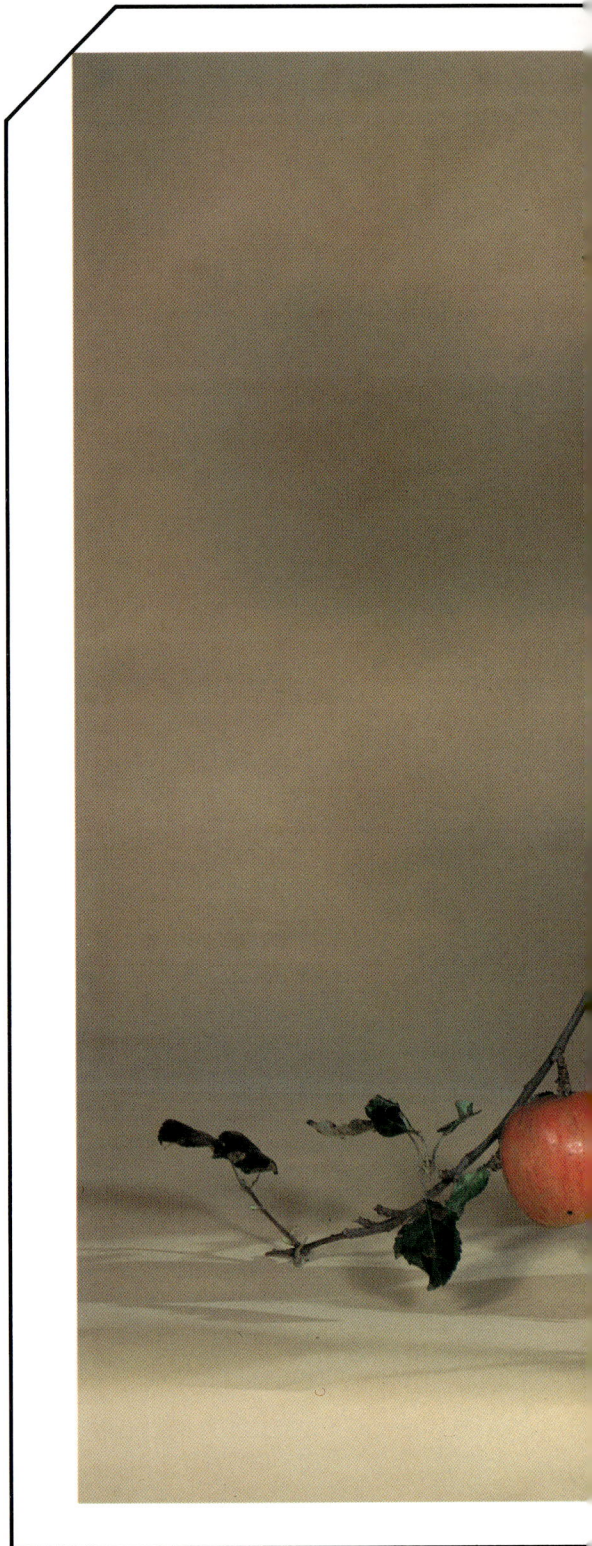

Both sides of the country road were lined with full blown *udo* blossoms. I felt as if I were on a white cloud as I kept walking in a dream-like state until eventually I found myself in front of an apple orchard. The green and red apples looked to me like cherubs playing on the branches and I felt as if I had wandered into a veritable fairyland.

Udo flower and apple in a basket and stand

One winter when I visited a snowy province I found an interesting persimmon branch from which all the fruit had fallen leaving only their dried calyxes. Luckily I was quite able to take any branches of my choice since the piled snow was a convenient foot stool. And when I brushed against the thick masses of snow along the path the boughs underneath released

of their heavy burden, sprang up to reveal fresh bright branches of Japanese cedar which were tipped with precious brown cones. They seemed to be trying to tell me that they were now wide awake.

Persimmon and Japanese cedar in "kanjiki" and snowshoes (straw)

Part II
FLOWERS
Beauty
in Rural Districts

Autumn fields can delight with unexpected views. Once I walked through a meadow and coming up over a hilltop saw beyond a mulberry field and a single plum tree. There on a plum branch for my special attention was a bird's nest. There is a saying that Japanese nightingales perch on plum trees. Could it have been a nightingale's nest? It did inspire me to make an arrangement to express the changing of the season from summer to fall. Was I successful using the lacey Chinese miscanthus with the casual informality of the stalks of cosmos? Perhaps not, but I only have to look at this picture to recapture the joy of that day.

Cosmos and Chinese miscanthus in a basket made of akebia

The double camellia with exquisite flowers was the center of admiration, not just for now but for weeks to come as each perfect bloom would be succeeded by another. Blooming at the same time in many of the farm villages were the graceful sprays of spirea covered all over with white florets so appropriately called in Japanese snow willow. The charming pictures these early spring flowering shrubs gave from the train windows helped lighten the hearts of the passengers.

Double camellia and spirea thunbergii in a rush basket

The snow camellia in the northern provinces waits desperately for the warmth of spring. When the sunshine comes and the snow thaws, the plant is striking. It is radiant with extremely fresh looking green leaves and scarlet blossoms, a joy for all.
Yukitsubaki *in a ceramic vase, Tokoname-yaki*

I will always remember these blossoms which, with a lovely smile, were blooming happily and vivaciously in the farm house garden. The carefree and fresh-looking blossoms and graceful branches remain as a very nice memory, especially with the sturdy silverleaf nodding playfully at the base of the peach tree.

The memory recalled when I heard "peach blossoms" reminds of the days when I was still a child. Is it because peach branches and rape flowers are arranged for the girls' festival on the third of March when the traditional Hina dolls are displayed?

Peach blossoms and Japanese silverleaf in a light brown ceramic vase, Tokoname-yaki

I always sense an indescribable fascination when I see plants that have endured through the severities of nature. The columbine is one of them; it is far stronger than plants that grow with the care and nurture of human hand. Its natural strength is what makes up its beauty.

When you use columbines for a flower arrangement, I believe, it is inevitable that you use a simple vase to go with them.
Columbine in a basket made of wisteria vine

The candle stand containing genista was probably used as a stand for the lamplight in olden times. I borrowed this stand from Akita (located in the northern part of Japan). The container of the barley, on the other hand, is an unforgettable rice tub I used every day at the countryside where I took refuge during the war.

"This is the barley I cultivated with so much care. I hope you will place these on the Buddhist alter in your house."—The barley was offered to me with these words, and I accepted them gratefully and almost tearfully. They created a rich atmosphere in the room in an instant, as well as dignity in the best sense of the word, which suddenly made the surrounding things insignificant.

The yellow color of the genista, which cheerfully colors farming villages, was remarkably bright, and I thought it would make a good companion for the aboundant barley.
Barley and genista in rice tub and candle stand

I was finally able to find deep-red ground cherries at the back of the barn of a farmhouse in the Tohoku district (northern part of Japan), and they were exactly what I had been looking for. They somehow reminded me of little urchins with apple-like cheeks playing hide-and seek. Their healthiness appealed to me as the sublime beauty fostered in nature.

The leaves of Japanese ginger grew vigorously, and looked as if they were taking a walk in groups.

Ground cherry and myōga leares (ginger family) in a ceramic vase

In making trips to hunt for new materials, the farming villages play the role of marvelous museums. Picture a man and wife absorbed in preparing seed beds. Or the neighborliness of the casual greetings of the passing people. Here was a field spread with horsebeam blossoms, radish flowers of white and purple, and the big round heads of spring onions and punctuating the pathways were clumps of bridal wreath and weeping forsythia. Thus the countryside continually entertains us.

Bridal wreath and weeping forsythia in brown and beige striped vase, Banko-yaki

It is such a peaceful feeling to find innocent-looking Japanese radish blossoms of light-purple and white blooming so serenely amid the bright yellow rape blossoms blooming powerfully in profusion.

It was such an afternoon as would make you feel as though the May wind were sending a contented voice saying, "What lovely weather!" I decided to use as the container a jar for pickles which never fails to evoke nostalgia for the many years I used it to make my household pickles.

Japanese radish blossoms and rape blossoms in a jar for pickles

Two years ago I was given this precious stool and the round straw lids with the explanation that a long time ago people used to put the straw lids on top of the stool as a cushion, and sat on it, and worked in the parallel position with the rice sprouts at the time of picking them up from the seedbed.

While being delighted to keep these folkcraft utensils, there is one issue that

never seems to leave my mind—the more I think about it, the more I get confused, because the mundane desire to create something splendid gets in the way.

And this is what I finally ended up with.

Rice sprouts and yellow iris in a stool (for transplanting rice) and round straw lids

The lilies of the valley, which were just starting to put forth buds when the parting with winter was drawing near, bear lots of leaves and white lovely flowers now when the breeze feels so nice.

The way the lilies of the valley bloom quietly, sending sweet fragrance appeared to be exactly like her flower meaning—happiness.

Lily of the valley in bamboo basket and straw boots

It was one moment in the afternoon of a certain autumn day when I was taking a walk through the beautiful countryside away from the city. There, I came across delicate, white carrot blossoms which looked like good silk. The way they swayed to the wind reminded me of white birds playing in the fields. And the large-flowered dahlias blooming abundantly in a variety of colors were suggestive of a scene of spectacular dance.

Carrot blossoms and dahlia in a Italian pot

In an neglected corner of the garden, kerria and hydrangeas were cheerfully heralding the early summer. I find hydrangeas fascinating throughout the year—very nice in winter and summer as well as in spring and fall.

They are absolutely exquisite in winter when they display the movement of the branches. They look daintier than ever after a snow when thin white ribbons outline the shape of the branches.

This arrangement looks quite natural—sort of like two congenial fellows after a visit to a hot springs. I was drawn to their conviviality.

They seemed to be trying to teach me how important it is to see things and people with unclouded eyes and open hearts.

Hydrangeas and kerria in a green pot, Tokoname-yaki

The sight of the rain-beaten St. John's-wort is so pathetic that it breaks my heart, and makes me want to try to figure out a way somehow to save it, whereas the breathtaking beauty of it on a sunny day is just incredible. I'm sure I am not the only one to get captivated by its gentle and charming appearance, which makes you think it is the way women should be.

The pure-white trumpet lilies are blooming so cleanly, and they look as if they see through our minds.

Today, I tried to convey the charm of farming villages through flowers.

St. John's-wort and white trumpet lilies in a bamboo basket

In Hachijo Island which is a little less then an hour's flight southwest of Tokyo, the trees such as fountain palm, date palm, and hemp palm add much grandeur to the scenery of the seaside. In reminiscence of a visit there I arranged freesia in a souvenir hat made of fountain palm bark. I think fondly of the freesia and strelitzia of Hachijo which bloom so casually all over the countryside.

Freesia in a fountain palm hat and fishing net

I happened to come across the garden peas and the beer barley when I was taking a walk near my house. What were they doing so far away from any garden just on a roadside of a street busy with traffic? Seeing them so unmindful of their setting they reminded me of children playing innocently and free of apprehensions.

I walked past them reluctantly, leaving this admonition, "Watch out for the passing cars, and do not ever get hurt!"
Beer barley and garden peas in vase and hemp yarn beam

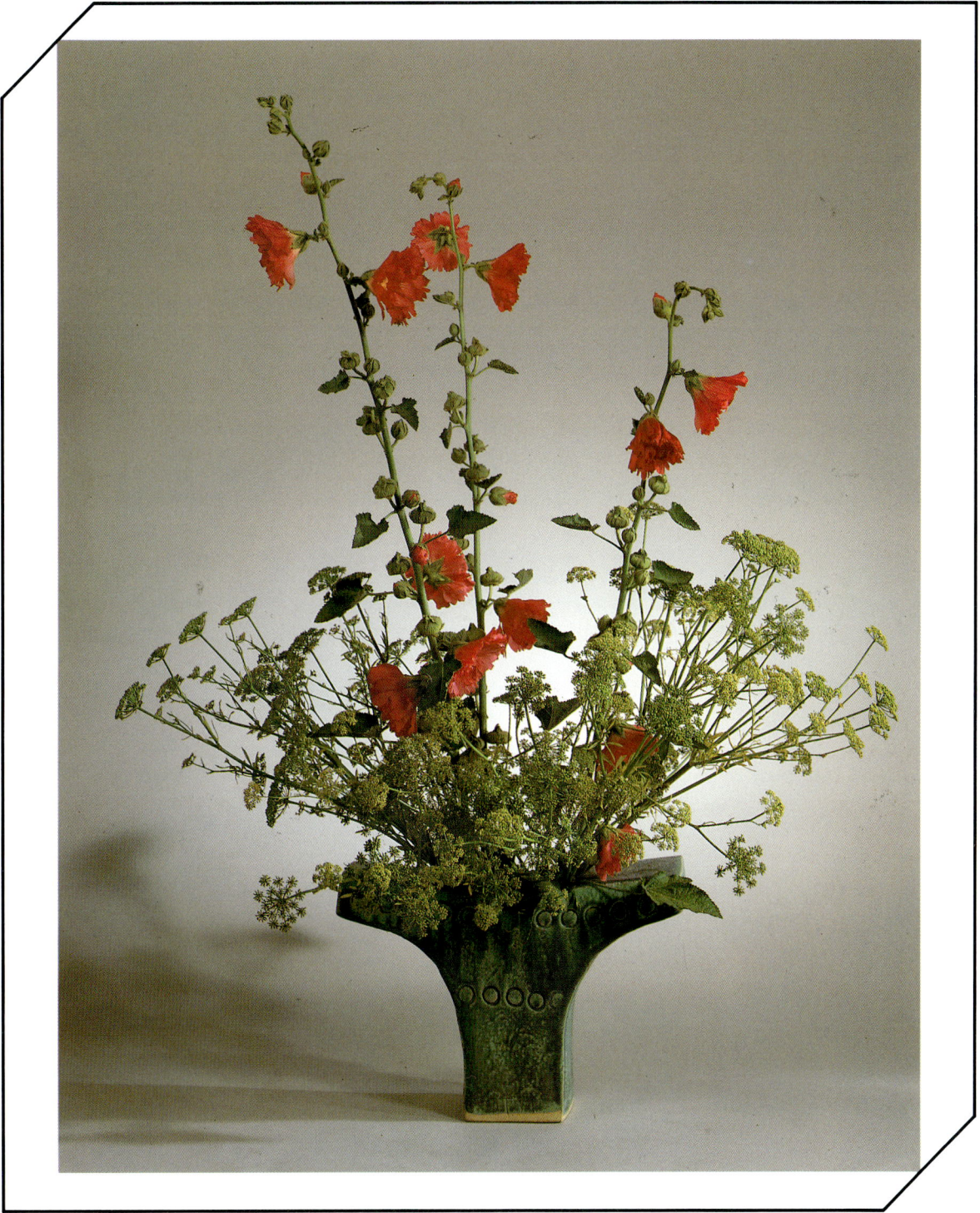

The hollyhock is one of the flower subjects which painters of Japanese pictures like to illustrate, and many fine examples are seen frequently in exhibitions.

When I see the old fashioned ones as well as the modern hollyhock blooming against a farmhouse on a hot summer day, it has an irresistable appeal for me.

The extra touch of the parsley flowers adds an unexpected elegance to the stately hollyhocks.
Hollyhock and parsley in a ceramic vase, Tokoname-yaki

Looking absolutely charming the seed pods from the thin branched beefsteak plant spread a delightful fragrance. Their interesting lines which could not be created artificially moved my imagination to help me create this combination, for the natural shape of the Transvaal

daisy complimented the movement of the linear materials.
Beefsteak plant seed poods and Transvaal daisy in a ceramic compote vase, Tokoname-yaki

"How lovely they must look under the moonlight!"—I could not help picturing such a sight as I stood in front of the buckwheat field, watching the white blossoms sway in unison to the slightest breeze.

I wonder what kind of stories the buckwheat and the gentian have to tell each other in the well-worn *neribachi* (a folkcraft utensil), which has a touch of warmth to it.

Buckwheat blossoms and gentian in a yellow ceramic vase, Seto-yaki

Quite a few cows were tethered on both sides of the cowbarn facing one another with a narrow aisle in between.

They acknowledged my presence by shifting their big bodies to cast sidelong glances at me. They were extremely sweet and their expressions seemed to say, "We all welcome you." But I was terribly nervous and had to pluck up courage to walk between them.

But what a reward when I came out at the opposite end of the dairy there was a mountain view so overwhelmingly romantic, that I could only blurt out "Idyllic."

Meadow grasses and red clover in a black vase, Banko-yaki

The climbing rose seemed to fascinate the passers-by with its red flowerets all over the hedge, which looked somewhat like a fully packed train.

The gently flowering carrot blossoms were doing their best to appear as beautiful as possible as the rose's partner, looking a bit concerned about the thorns of the rose.

The combination of red and white colors is always such a lovely sight to watch.

Climbing rose and carrot blossoms in a container

The leaf, colored heavily with autumnal tints, is just about to say a last farewell to its vine. Fully flowering Chinese miscanthus moving quietly like fleecy clouds in the sky contrasts beautifully against the setting sun. As the wind sweeps past the Chinese miscanthus and shakes the plant to and fro tufts glisten and give off a silver ray.

Autumn has painted a uniquely different picture in the vineyard.
Chinese miscanthus in a navy-blue vase, Kyo-yaki

The white, graceful spikes of the miscanthus were ornamenting the field, and there, the subdued color of the frostbitten flowers and leaves of the hydrangea displayed a wonderful splendor along with the spikes of the miscanthus. Together, they struck me as extremely

beautiful. The whole scene seemed to give me some idea as to how we should "age" gracefully, an issue imposed upon human beings.
Chinese miscanthus and hydrangea in a Li dynasty vase

It has become a practice every year to deflect the heat of the summer sun by planting gourds on a reed screen. At the end of season the leaves withered leaving gourds on the roof. Collecting a few and some of the dried vines I brought them into the house to enjoy them as a decoration.
Gourd and its vine with dried gourd vine

The China aster we come across at the countryside fascinates me so much especially because of its color and its waywardness—the way it blooms wildy all over. The amaranthus caudatus, on the other hand, kept company with the China aster, looking absolutely composed.

I fondly remember the way the two, which were so expressive, beautifully ornamented the late summer field.

China aster and amaranthus caudatus in a hemp yarn beam

It was delightful to arrange these materials in a much used cooking utensil. I could even savor the warm smell of freshly boiled rice cooked with red beans.

The old custom of delivering to neighbors and friends lacquer boxes of red rice with a bit of nandina leaves, salt, and toasted sesame and crepe wrappers decorating the boxes seems to have changed over the years. But to those of us who belong to that earlier generation the ritual holds a heart warming tenderness.

Adzuki (red) beans and nandina in a basket steamers (seiro)

The carrots left unharvested, produced the lace-like blossoms all over the field completely transforming its former appearance.

The rows of beer barley just before the harvest created some poetical sentiments with their heads looking exactly like golden needles under the blue sky. I was simply overwhelmed by the unfathomable beauty of the countryside, and could only stand there without words.
Carrot blossoms and beer barley in a stool for transplanting rice

In winter after the mulberry leaves have been picked or fallen away, the branches are neatly bundled with straw rope for the cold season. Seeing them trussed you know that the farming villages are prepared for the vigors of the winter months. At the base of the mulberries the amur adonis begin putting forth their buds so that they will be fully open to celebrate the New Year's festivities.
Adonis amurensis and mulberry tree in a black round basin

Oh, look, a garden of buckwheat with pristine white flowers all swaying on slim stalks as thin as an egret's legs.

One day those buckwheat blossoms may be transformed into a tasty sauce to add flavor for guests on some social event.

But this one moment in autumn makes me lose count of time while the image of buckwheat fields becomes indelible in my mind.

Buckwheat blossoms in a bamboo basket and lacquered hot water pail

Part III
VEGETABLES
The Triumph
of Vegetables

Are these really the same as the prim looking brussels sprouts at the stores wrapped up in the vinyl bags? It is simply unthinkable because they look so different in the field. Until this day, I have seen the brussel sprouts under three different conditions.

The first time was in Fukushima (a prefecture about 130 miles north of Tokyo). I came across a lovely sight of them protecting the children under the snow with long leaves. The second time was in Shizuoka (a prefecture about 100 miles southwest of Tokyo), and the frostbitten leaves of brussels sprouts bore a striking resemblance to the Japanese brocade cloth.

As for this time, it was somehow painfully impressive to see them without the brocade outfit and with a lot of children. It looks as though they tried to have as many children as they possibly could for our sake.

Daffodils, with their pretty flowers, were ornamenting the stages of spring one after another.

Brussels sprouts and daffodils in a brown ceramic basin, Banko-yaki

A sense of the season—it is a marvelous gift given to us by nature. It never fails to humble and gives us peace of mind. This combination of materials seem to be most compatible. I like the way the well-rounded pussy willows shine like silver and how the cabbage left in the field insists on sprouting into yellow flowers. And do not miss the standing leeks dragging trousers of withered leaves.

Leek, pussy willow and Chinese cabbage in a ceramic vase, Banko-yaki

I happened to find these cabbages soon after I decided to take up the flower arrangement based on farming villages, and started travelling here and there to hunt for the materials. These two cabbages were left all alone and were sitting primly in the big field, as if they had been waiting for me.

At that time, I was struggling for better ways to arrange farm products, and this piece of work with the cabbages was the very first satisfactory one for me.

The beautiful color of the leaves and the deep impression I felt when I touched the sturdy figures still remain vividly in my hands.

Cabbages and their blossoms in a blue basin, Seto-yaki

The celery, full-grown with abundant leaves, was now ready for the harvest. It looked magnificent and so different from the ones we find at the stores. I was so overwhelmed by its appearance that it did not occur to me to make an ikebana piece with it. When I returned from the celery field, a yellow dahlia was waiting for me at the gate of the inn I was staying. The picture of it lingered on in my mind, and I decided to keep the memory of that day in a photograph along with the celery.

Lovely ribbed skin, refreshing fragrant green leaves—everything about celery is too nice

to end up as only an object to satisfy one's appetite. Consider, the stalks of celery might be waiting quietly in the refrigerator for just a chance to please you when you make a flower arrangement.

Celery and dahlia in a bamboo basket

The celery never fails to give pleasant thoughts to people with its soft, light-green leaves, refreshing fragrance, and with its perfect texture.

I decorated an evening table with the celery and the beautifully colored gerbera. Thanks to the charm of the celery which makes a delicious dish even more tasty, I was able to have such a wonderful time tonight.

Celery and gerbera in a bamboo basket

These stalks, which are called *hong-tsai-tai* and are often used for cooking, were glossy, purple-colored and looked absolutely healthy.

The purple color fades further up the stalks, and there towards the top, a bunch of tiny yellow flowers were blooming like a swarm of butterflies flying in the air.

By grace of the rich soil, the pale green color of butterhead lettuces looked beautiful, and they had such soft, fair skin which might get broken by a heedless touch.

Hong-tsai-tai and butterhead lettuces in earthern pot and tupper ware boxes

The big, round onion heads in the field had an air of perfect composure but the magnolia blossoms above them seemed threatened by the merciless buffeting by the winds of spring. The survival strength of the magnolias is amazing but my heart is still pained by the pathetic picture of the magnolia blossoms trying desperately not to be blown away.
Onion head and lily magnolia in a basket, made in China

In the humble vegetable garden of our house, I one day found some sweet flowers I had never seen before. They were purple-red flowerets.

I later learned that they were the burdock blossoms, and come to think of it, I fortunately got to see them because I had not taken good care of the garden. I had been so lazy, but I felt as if fortune had visited me without my being aware of it.

Burdock blossoms and tomato in a porcelain vase, Kyo-yaki

What a surprise! A small but bright red rose was blooming in the corner of a field of cucumbers which were just starting to bear fruit.

They seemed to say to each other, "Let's try and get through this summer heat together."
Cucumber and rose in a bamboo strainer (bowl) and bamboo tube

In the working place which is deliberately sheltered from the sun, an elderly couple were sorting the straight-shaped cucumbers from the crooked cucumbers.

And in the front yard hung a bunch of bright-red, fat tomatoes clutching on to the "hand" delightfully under the bright sunlight, and looking ready to burst.

The soil, which is the result of tremendous devotion, has transformed them into the actual rich appearance of the present.

The taste of a freshly picked tomato—to me, there is nothing quite like it in the whole world.
Tomatoes and sunflowers in a well bucket

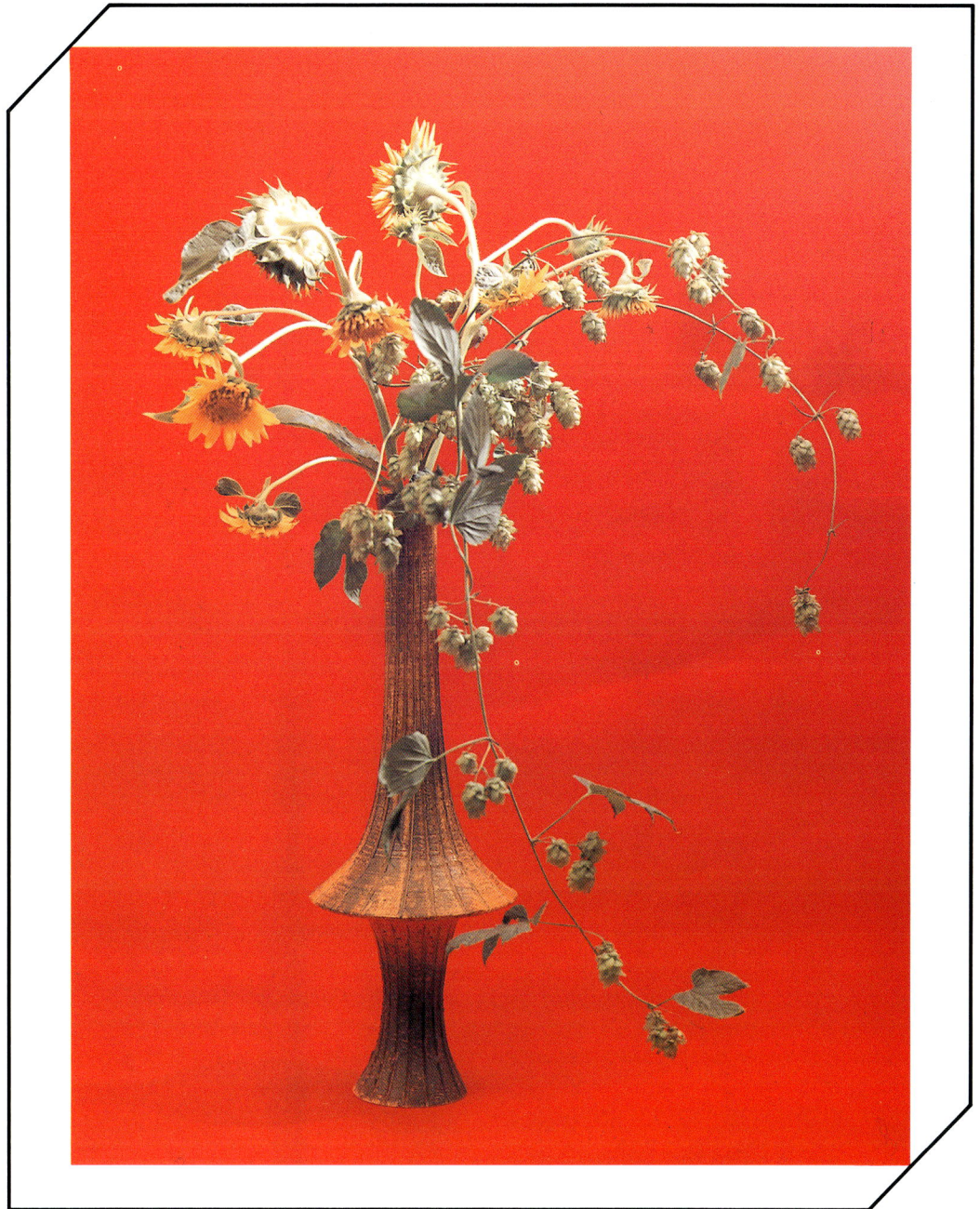

Long ago in the Babylonian kingdom, there lived a king who was a very stouthearted man, but at the same time, he was such a devoted husband. The beautiful queen was the princess of Media, a country in the north.

The queen, having been brought up in a mountainous country, grew weak both mentally and physically because of the bright sun of the Mesopotamian plain, and felt a never-ceasing yearning for her home country.

The legend has it that the king, in an effort to console the queen made an artificial reproduction of the green mountains of her home country Media in the palace. It is said that the hanging garden in Babylon is the one, and that in this dream garden were planted the hops which the queen adored.

What a beautiful love story! I, too, can easily picture the magic-like charm of hops anytime, anywhere.

Hops and sunflowers in a brown porcelain vase, Kiyomizu-yaki

A couple of small white florets seized my attention and I wondered what they were. My hostess told me, "These are volunteer buckwheat blossoms. You are welcome to take these if you like."

I was fortunate also to get these irregularly formed asparagus.

The resultant work was a happy reminder of a day of successful material hunting when I was able to hold in my arms the Oriental buckwheat and the Western asparagus at the same moment.

Buckwheat blossoms and asparagus in a blue and white striped oblong basin, Kiyomizu-yaki

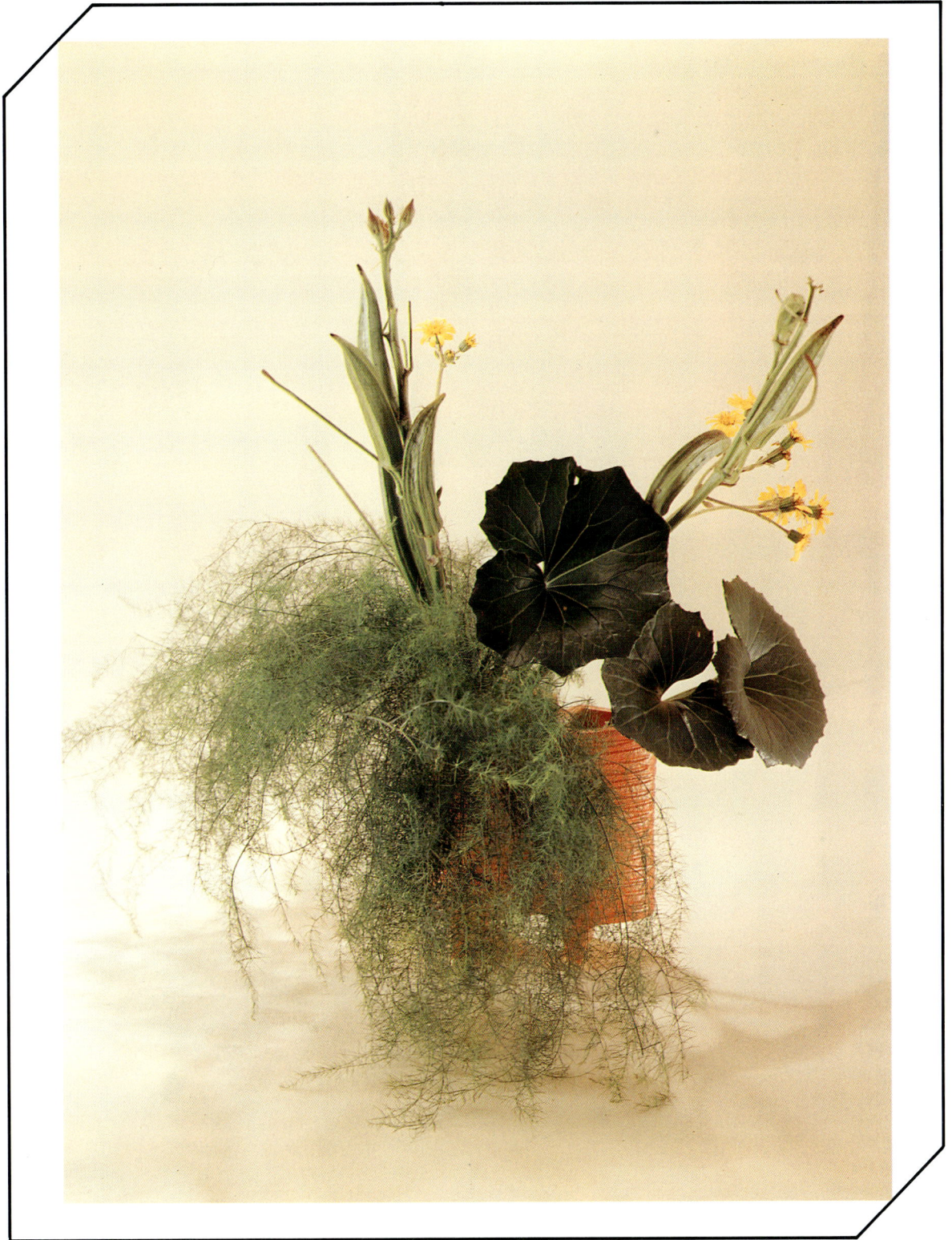

It is amazing how those gentle flowers of okra produce the vegetable for all the world to enjoy its special taste. The fairy-like leaves of fern are what the asparagus stalks turn into when they are left unharvested in the fields.

I am sending you one page of early fall, feeling strongly that I am here alone enjoying the beautiful changes of nature.

Okra, dwarf asparagus leaves, and Japanese silver leaves in a vermilion vase, Banko-yaki

I tried to express through this ikebana piece the image of a scene—people of a farming village engaged in a difficult work of digging the lotus roots, without damaging them, in the cold, wintry wind. Lotus roots are considered to be very propitious because you can supposedly see far into the future through the small holes.

I put in some narcissus to create the atmosphere of the New Year.

Lotus root, dried matteuccia orientalis and narcissus in a yellow basin, Banko-yaki

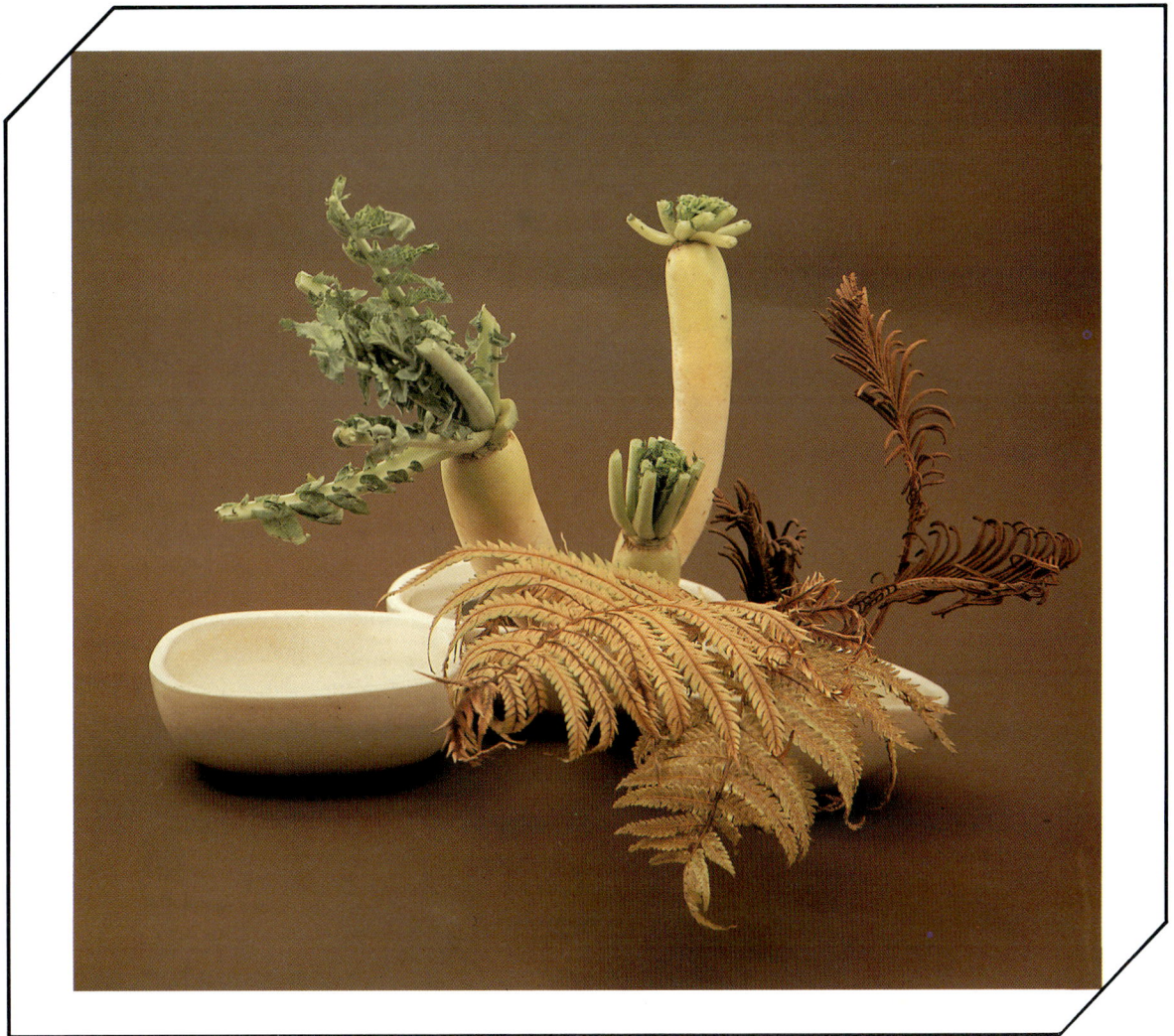

The long, large variety of white radish is a very familiar vegetable to the Japanese people. Its shape is descriptive of a girl's legs which are rather excessively developed giving rise to the term "radish legs." There are however many varieties of the radish, so for change, why not enjoy a slender one in ikebana?
Giant white radish and dried fern in three ceramic bowls

"Look how healthy we are!" say these turnips bursting with vitality. "Attention, where are you going now," they demand.

But the Japanese pink *sasa*-lily just gently looks on and is silent.

Turnips, soybeans and sasa-*lily in a ceramic vase, Banko-yaki*

Left after the harvesting, I saw laying on the ground some broad beans all withered and weakened. As another work of nature, they appeared so beautiful to me that my heart was deeply enchanted. Without thinking I picked up the broad beans and took them home with me to make a flower arrangement using them along

with some gorgeous gold-banded lilies. As the broad beans came back to life, they exhibited their own beauty matching that of the lilies.

Broad bean and gold-banded lily in a ceramic vase, Banko-yaki

The moment I dug them up pulling out the whole plant, pink root and all, a marvelous ginger aroma filled the air. How like a new born red faced baby the roots appear! The withered *udo* blossoms were added just for contrast of the old with the new.

Ginger and udo blossoms in a ceramic bowl

The garden peas can be missed easily unless we look carefully for the full pods are hiding quietly under the shade of the leaves. My stiff heart seemed to unwind gradually by watching the gentle way the beautiful garden pea blossoms of white and purple trail the tendrils which appeared to keep growing rapidly and endlessly.

The bright red color of the red radish has made this ikebana brighter and more delightful.
Garden peas and red radish in a basket with a handle

The farm products placed in the stores are totally without spirit, whereas the ones freshly picked in farming villages look lively and full of energy. They appear to me exactly like children playing around and having fun climbing up and down the hills. I arranged the onions with the idea that they are playing on the straw.

Onion and aster with straw rope

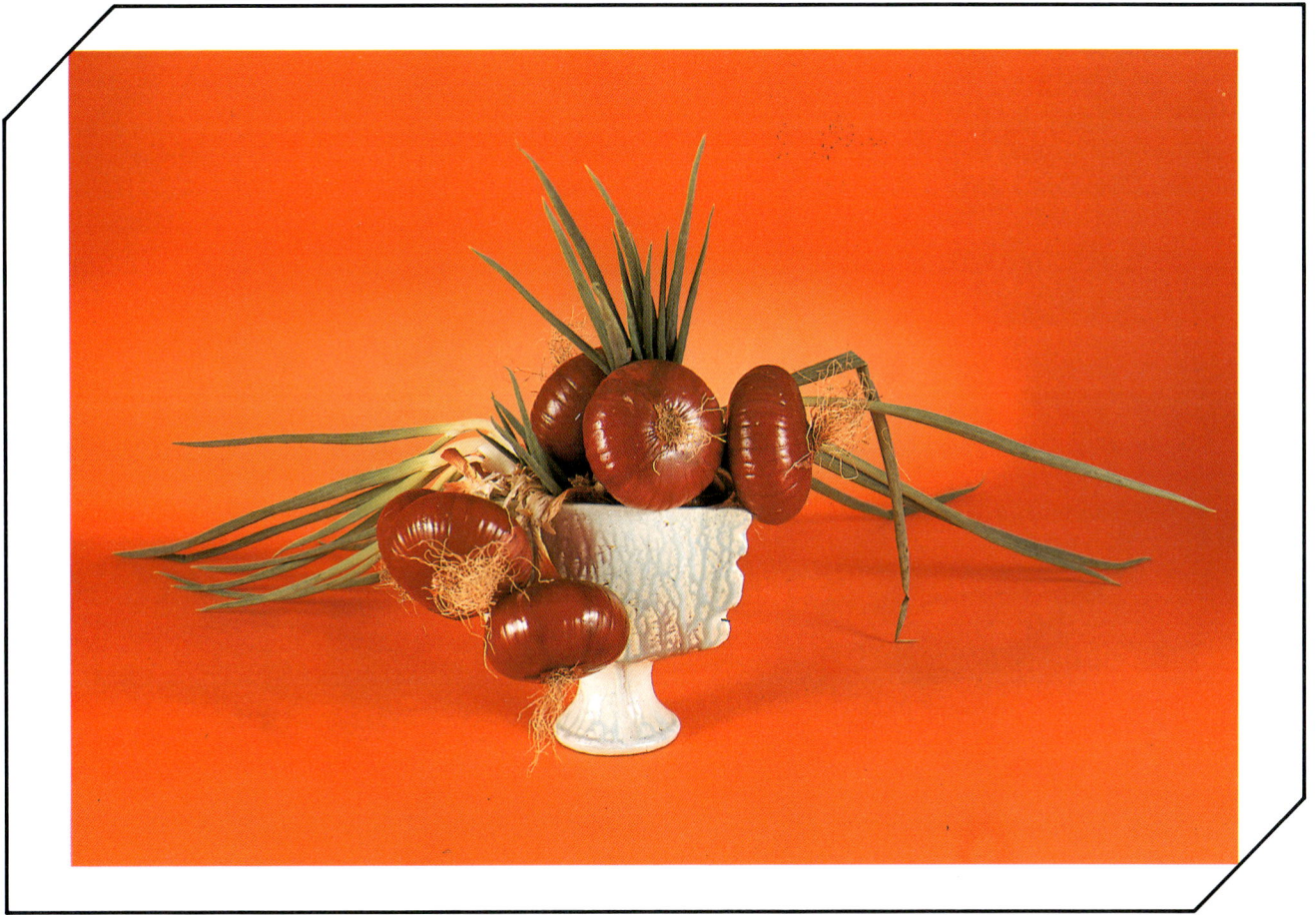

When I travel to the farm villages and am presented with the choicest of their current crops, I never fail to be tempted to use some of them in an ikebana. Here I peeled the outer skin off the red onions to reveal a burst of brilliant color. So lovely and attractive was the color that it made you want to fix your eyes on it.

Red onion in a ceramic vase, Tokoname-yaki

In the farm house in Aizu (a district in the western part of Fukushima Prefecture), it was dark even in the daytime, but I was warmly received with smoldering pieces of wood burning in the hearth. And there from the ceiling hung incredibly beautiful, golden yellow corncobs. They were indeed "a glorious chandelier by the fireside."

The natural color of dried-up cornhusks, too, was a beauty beyond all description.

I was told that "These are going to be the feed for birds," and when I left the farm house, embracing two or three of the precious corncobs, I found that the village had turned into a fairyland-like silver world all covered with snow.
Corncobs, roses of sharon, and cypress in a white vase

Sesame stalks are harvested each year and put to dry under the eaves of the farm houses. They have always challenged my imagination. How to use them? After many failures I was satisfied finally with this attempt. The shaggy mums are an interesting contrast for the rough texture of the sesame stalks.

Sesame pods and small spider chrysanthemums in a white ceramic vase, Banko-yaki

There is a saying that one can cultivate patience by eating the burdock. As if to verify the saying, pleasant strength is felt from the burdock. Almost as soon as I arranged the burdock, the stalk began to put forth small sprouts which in no time grew into leaves, and thus demonstrated the excellent vigor.

The big, red pimiento is very well-matched with the burdock, which made it possible for me to produce a powerful piece.

Burdock stalk and red pimiento in a ceramic vase, Shigaraki-yaki

Above the ground taro, sometimes called Elephant ears, has large fresh looking leaves, but there is a completely different and wonderful subterranean world to it. How wonderful to see nature's creation so remarkably and beautifully balanced.
Taro potato in a ceramic vase, Shigaraki-yaki

The garlic stems were exhausted from exerting all their energies to producing fat bulbs. Their extremely thin stems could no longer hold erect their cone shaped caps and they collapsed one after the other to the ground. At their side, the bright yellow and orange, strong looking marigolds were flowering as if to soothe the tired garlic plants.

Garlic and marigold in a basket with a handle

The chic Japanese toad lily is occasionally used as a flower for the tea ceremony, but its natural beauty as seen in the fields and mountains is something special. What stopped me as I was taking a walk was the withered flower of hydrangea which still looked lovely. I also found bunches of young fresh spring onions standing in a row looking as if they were making hand—like entreaties to the passers-by. It was such a casual but enjoyable encounter in a quiet spot of a mountain village.

Japanese toad lily, spring onion, and hydrangea in a ceramic vase, Banko-yaki

Among the carrots dug up from the field, there can be found from time to time some perfectly shaped for my sort of ikebana. This carrot is one of them. It is of course no good for greengrocers, but instead they are loved, cherished, and Tarranged by people as an interesting ikebana material.

The meek cosmos flowers bending themselves to the wind here and there in the vast expansion of the fields seemed to soothe my mind.

Carrot and cosmos in a ceramic vase, Banko-yaki

Sweet potatoes have many memories for me. As a child I was allowed to dig them on visits to the family farm. In winter when the sweet potato vendor shouted his wares, I would run out to his cart to buy a hot roasted goodie. And my favorites at the cake shop were always

the sweet potato cakes.

    These with their vines still attached I dug up today unmindful of the muddy field.

Sweet potato in a ceramic vase, Shigaraki-yaki

Onions, which bestow mysterious taste and mysterious power upon us, may be a vitamin for daily life.

Some onions are hanging happily and leisurely under the eaves of our house, enjoying the scenery around them until the day when they can be of service. Some are forced into net bags at the stores in big cities, and get fumbled with and bumped, with no choice at all. I just cannot help feeling deeply touched by such different phases of destiny. Around that time, I met a pussy willow by the old well in our back yard. She had big, silver-colored, vacant eyes.

Oh, why are you here at this time of the year, looking this way? I asked her about the mystery within myself.

It was a cold, wintry day.

Onions and pussy willows in a dark blue Iwata glass

A bulky bundle wrapped in the newspaper was given to me with the words—this is for you. The contents I found were red peppers with black, wrinkled, completely withered leaves. After a painstaking and time-consuming work of removing all the leaves, there appeared an elegant figure of red peppers.

You might think "elegant" is not the appropriate word to describe red peppers, but I am convinced that you will agree with me if you take a look at this picture. Such an elegant stem structure of the red peppers, absolutely unimaginable from the original state. I must say that after tolerating severe weather and undergoing extraordinary ordeals of mother nature, the red peppers have indeed achieved a triumph.

Red peppers and Japanese silver leaves in a light-green compote, Banko-yaki

These freeze-dried bean curds tasted absolutely delicious.

I tried to express a farming village in a cold province by arranging the winter vegetable in the straw shoes a special product of Iwate Prefecture (located in the northern part of Japan), along with the freeze-dried bean curd.

The homespun *sakiori* of which I am so proud was given to me and I am happy to use it on the table for special occasions.
Leek, dropwort, and freeze-dried bean curd in a straw shoes and sakiori *(a fabric with thinly ripped cloth woven into it)*

The peanuts are much loved and used by people of all generations as relish, snack, and as a cooking material. It has been my longstanding wish to utilize them as a flower arrangement material.

These peanuts were piled up under the eaves of a farm house seemingly dirty and completely unobtrusive, which made me wonder, are these really peanuts?

I still vividly remember how springy my steps were as I headed homeward, after my long-cherished desire had been materialized. I gave so much thought to what I should choose as their companion, but eventually I selected the white-cedar leaves which I happened to find at the gate of the same farm house.
Peanuts and white-cedar leaves in a pot, Soma-yaki

There is nothing better than the just plain boiled noodles in the cold season because it warms up every part of your body.

A lot of traditional things tend to get replaced by new things nowadays, but this container stays on in the traditional form as if it thinks it only natural. The people still cherish it and find it quite useful, and I, too, am impressed with the fineness of it.

I would like you to take a look at this arrangement as one of the examples which utilize folkcraft utensils.

Wheat and noodles in lacquered box and handmade bamboo strainer

Winter sweet was blooming quietly under a still chilly air, and its yellow and transparent blossoms gave out noble fragrance.

Sarcandra glabra was swaying under the green leaves, looking somewhat like a lighted red lamp.

In order to fully enjoy the beautiful natural tone of color, I decided to put Japanese honey locust pods around the container to accentuate the piece because they still look pretty even after they are withered. *Winter sweet and sarcandra glabra in a bamboo basket around the dried Japanese honey locust dried Japanese honey locust*

In the snowy provinces, they celebrate the New Year for the second time on January 15. They wait until the branches of the dogwood get red, and then they make dumplings of five colors, stick them onto the branches, and decorate the rooms with them. I understand there also is another custom, and that is to form the straw into the shape of rice sprouts, and as a way to pray for a good harvest, stick them into the snow-covered garden for the neighbors who come to celebrate the New Year together. I wonder if it is one of the wisdoms of life which helps with these kind of events to light up as much as possible the hearts of the people which threaten to get depressed during the long, snowbound wintering.

The blossoms made of rice cake in a Nambu iron tea kettle

Suggestions for Ikebana

It has always been the principle of my ikebana life that one can use any material he likes and arrange it as freely as his heart guides him, without being forced or restricted by the doctrines of other people. Beginners, when they hear this, might feel helpless and not know where to start. I'd like to say to them: "Just give it a try and practice as often as possible." Only through numerous trials your technical hand and your artistic eye will be trained, which will lead to the achievement of truly creative and individual work.

The merit of this method is that you can give full play to your imagination and experience in it the pleasure of artistic expression to your heart's content. I believe, this is the very essence of the art of ikebana.

The arrangement on the left side was done by a pupil who tried ikebana for the first time. The same material, already cut for the said arrangement by this pupil, was used by me to produce a completely different example which is shown on the right side. You can see that the same material handled by different hands results in various forms and expressions.

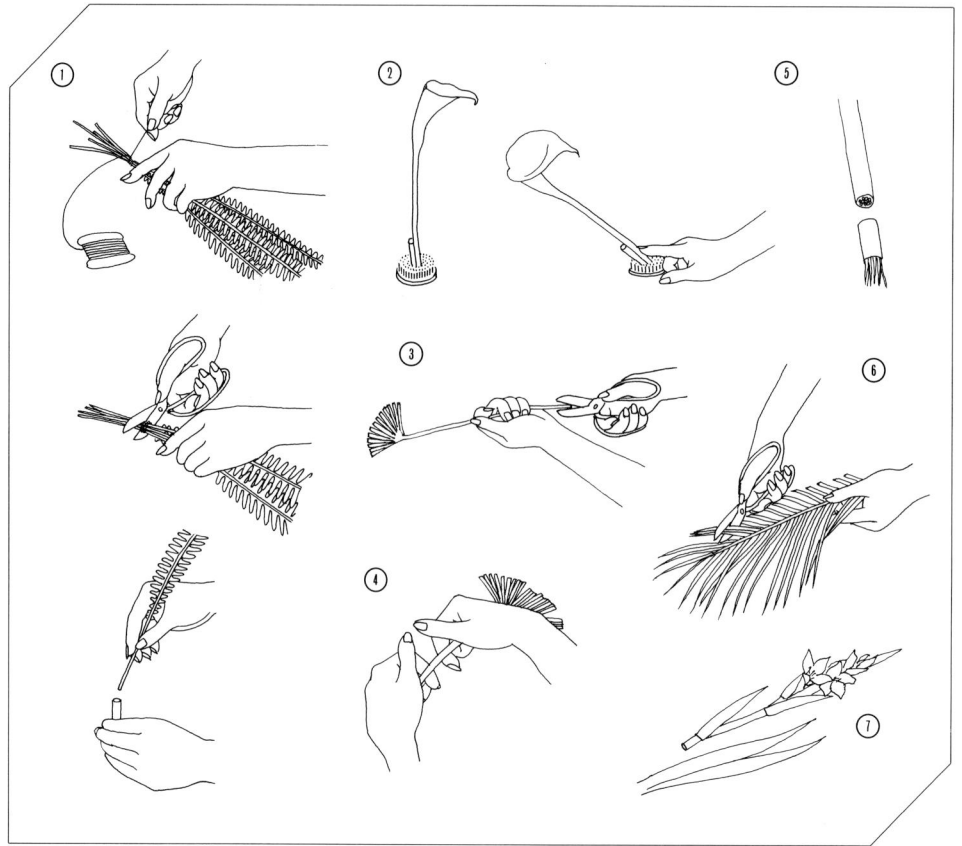

Flower Materials Hard to Handle

1. **Thin and hard stems difficult to stand on the needlepoint holder (e.g. *tamashida*, fern):** Make a rather thick bundle by bringing some stems together, and bind it. Cut the bundle just under the bound part, and stand it on the needlepoint holder.

   When you want to stand a single stem, first prepare a rather thick and soft stem. Stick your stem into the prepared one and stand the latter on the needlepoint holder.

2. **Stems so soft that they guickly begin to fall when stood on the needlepoint holder (e.g. calla lily):** Apply some soft stems of the same kind to your stems and let them stand on the needlepoint holder by supporting their lower part only. Incline the stems in the desired direction by heavily pushing their base only.

3. **How to stand a hard stem on the needlepoint holder (e.g. hemp palm):** Cut the stem at the base in two or in the form of a cross, and stand it on a the needlepoint holder vertically. Incline it in the desired direction by heavily pushing the base only.

4. **How to bend a branch:** Bend the branch carefully by holding it in the palms of your hands, as if you were warming it.

5. **How to stand a hollow stem on the needlepoint holder (e.g. amaryllis):** Make the hollow stem solid by stuffing it with materials such as straw. Cut the stuffed stem so as to ensure a smooth section before standing it on the needlepoint holder.

6. **How to handle leaf materials (e.g. date palm):** In the case of arranging a Canary Island date palm and some such materials, first trim the leaves properly so that some neatness will be lent to the material. Then the harmony of the work will be easily secured.

7. **How to handle materials with heavy flowers (e.g. gladiolus):** Separate the gladiolus stems into those with flowers and those with leaves before arranging them. Handle freesia, iris, tulip, etc. in the same way.